United States
Department of
Agriculture

Forest Service

FS-880

July 2007

USDA Forest Service Strategic Plan FY 2007–2012

Contents

From the Chief

The Forest Service, building on achievements gained through a century of commitment to excellence, continues its stewardship of the Nation's forests and grasslands to sustain natural resources for current and future generations.

This plan provides the strategic direction that guides the Forest Service in delivering its mission. We address the core principles by which we work; major issues currently important to natural resources management and to the strategic goals upon which the agency will focus for fiscal years (FY) 2007 through 2012. Our programs and budget are aligned with the goals and objectives in this strategic plan and as well as with our focus areas. Our strategic direction supplements the USDA Strategic Plan for FY 2005–2010 in delivery of the Department's mission.

Through State foresters, tribal leaders, and other partners, we provide financial and technical assistance to help forest landowners, public and private, manage their lands for sustainability. Our International Programs staff provides worldwide resource expertise, helping to promote global sustainable natural resource management.

We recognize that some of the work we do and services we provide can be hazardous. My central concern, as Chief, is that we always maintain the highest levels of safety for employees and the public. No job done or no service delivered is so important that it cannot be done safely.

As you read this document, we invite you to look for ways in which you can help us with conservation and stewardship of the Nation's forests and grasslands. This is not a solitary journey—we seek your assistance. Together, we can help the Nation remain connected to its natural resource heritage.

Abigail R. Kimbell, Chief

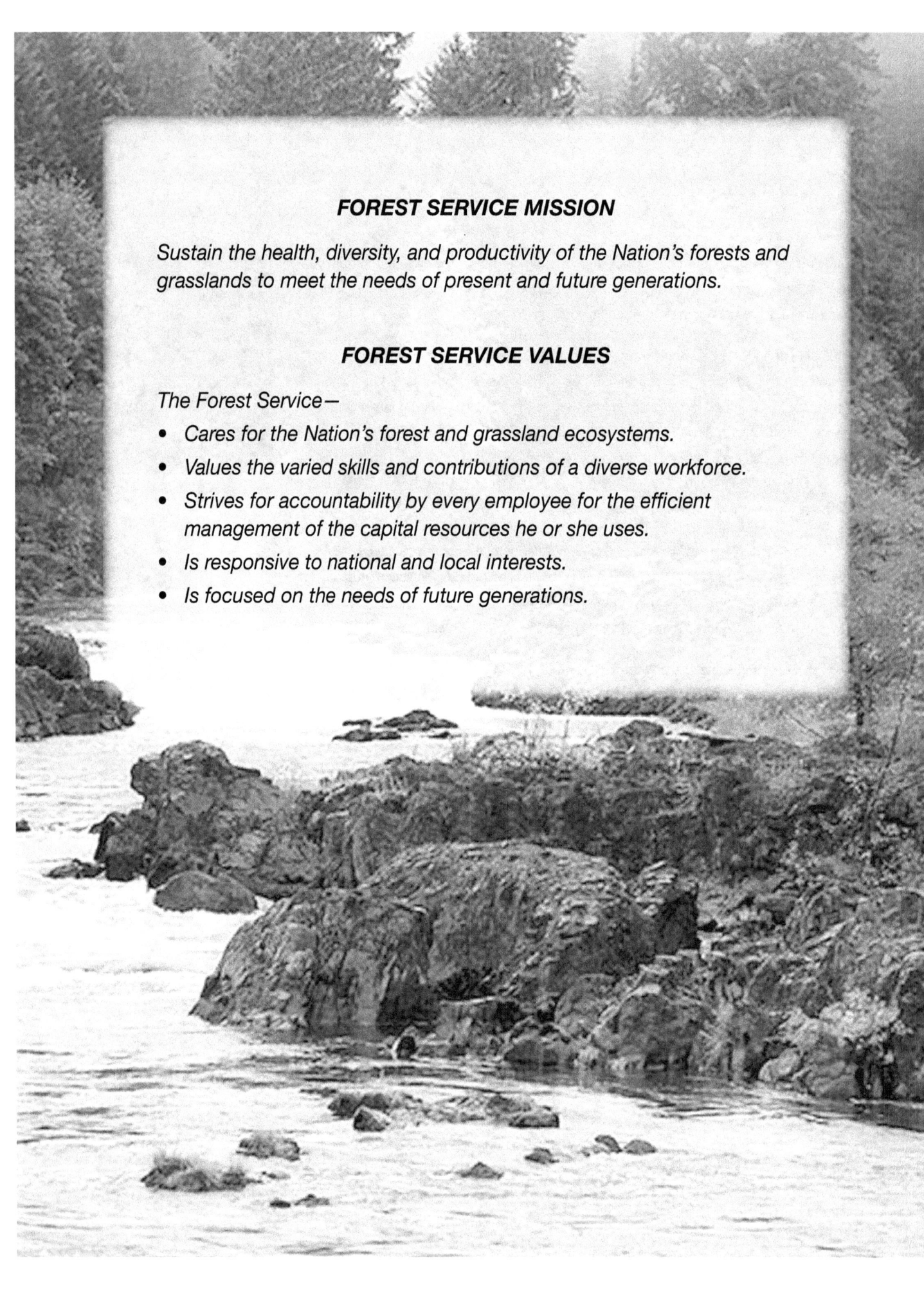

FOREST SERVICE MISSION

Sustain the health, diversity, and productivity of the Nation's forests and grasslands to meet the needs of present and future generations.

FOREST SERVICE VALUES

The Forest Service—

- *Cares for the Nation's forest and grassland ecosystems.*
- *Values the varied skills and contributions of a diverse workforce.*
- *Strives for accountability by every employee for the efficient management of the capital resources he or she uses.*
- *Is responsive to national and local interests.*
- *Is focused on the needs of future generations.*

Management Principles

Managing the natural resources of the Nation's forests and grasslands requires the complex integration of resource assessments, management actions, and cooperative partnerships.

United States population growth and expanding urban centers have created a greater demand for goods, services, and amenities from the Nation's private and public forests and grasslands. Given such changes, this section addresses core principles and issues central to delivering the Forest Service's mission.

Increasingly diverse urban populations are losing their awareness and knowledge of the natural systems on which they depend. The Forest Service, U.S. Department of Agriculture (USDA), must connect with and educate these citizens to expand their understanding of the links between people, the way they live, and the natural settings within which they live.

With increasingly urbanized landscapes, emergency response—including fighting wildland fires—becomes more complex and challenging. Along with our partners, the Forest Service is committed to maintaining and fielding a safe, effective response organization that can be mobilized for managing wildland fires or other national emergencies. We are jointly committed to reducing the loss of life and property and maintaining landscape values. Together, we will invest in the personnel, training, and equipment and provide leadership commensurate with those responsibilities.

Sustaining the Nation's Natural Resources

To achieve sustainability—the capacity of forests and grasslands to maintain their health, productivity, diversity, and overall integrity—the agency will integrate environmental, social, and economic issues and values into its management decisions and actions while accounting for future as well as present needs.

We will continue our commitment to reducing *threats* to the Nation's forests and grasslands. These threats include (1) the risk of loss from catastrophic wildland fire caused by hazardous fuel buildup; (2) the introduction and spread of invasive species; (3) the loss of open space and resulting fragmentation of forests and grasslands that impairs ecosystem function; and (4) unmanaged recreation, particularly the unmanaged use of off-highway vehicles. During this next strategic planning cycle, the agency will maintain its focus on mitigating these threats through its natural resource programs and through collaborative efforts with other agencies, States, tribes, local communities, and other pertinent partners.

In addition to sustaining damage caused by natural disturbances, most national forests and grasslands in the United States have been affected by human activities. Forest and grassland *restoration* will help reestablish structural characteristics, native species, and ecological processes. Active management is often required to achieve ecosystem restoration objectives, and income from commercial uses of natural resources may be used to help fund restoration activities. Forest Service managers use the best available science to understand and mitigate the causes of environmental damage. They use techniques such as reintroduction of natural fire regimes where appropriate and safe to do so, removal of invasive species, thinning of overly dense forest stands, and seeding with native plant species. The agency's commitment to restoring the functional resiliency of forests and grasslands to resist disturbance and change is the foundation of its management.

The Forest Service recognizes the value of incorporating environmental stewardship into its daily business operations. Measuring, managing, and reducing individual and collective consumption of energy and materials will help the agency reduce its ecological impact.

The Earth's *climate* is undergoing a period of relatively rapid change both in temperature and in the variability of climate patterns. Climate change will impact forest, range, and human well-being by potentially altering the ability of ecosystems to provide life-supporting goods and services. The implication for natural resource management is to be flexible and adapt management strategies to help mitigate the effects of climate change. In short, we need to develop new knowledge so that we can manage for future change, ensuring the continued provision of goods, services, and values from forests and rangelands.

International Engagement: Improving Natural Resource Management Overseas and in the United States

The Forest Service works to improve policies and practices of natural resource management around the world, which not only advances the sustainability of those critical resources but also improves resource conditions here at home. It is important for the agency to stay abreast of the international trends that shape natural resource policies and management of the Nation's forests as well as trade in forest products. The increasing interconnectedness of global ecological, social, and economic forces dictate the necessity of the agency to remain connected with partners who need its help in some areas and who can also offer it innovations and tools that could advance its goals. Specific reasons to stay involved internationally include the following:

- *Adjusting to changing global economic realities.* Understanding changes regarding trade in wood and wood products will improve natural resource management on U.S. private and public lands, as well as assist associated industries.

- *Improving the competitiveness of working U.S. forests through lessons learned overseas.* The Forest Service can improve forest production, competitiveness, and efficiency by supporting the development and marketing of new forest products and processes.

- *Leveling the playing field for U.S. industry.* The Forest Service helps level the playing field for natural resources goods and services by combating illegal logging and promoting sustainable forest management overseas.

- *Learning about market-based innovations from other nations.* Other nations can provide potential lessons for the United States; for example, in the development of markets for ecosystem services.

- *Understanding climate change internationally.* Tracking climate changes that occur overseas can inform U.S. policy and help develop new markets for mitigation strategies, such as carbon sequestration.

- *Protecting against invasive species.* The expansion of global markets leads to the distribution of pests beyond their natural habitat, both into and out of the United States. Forest Service scientists work with their international counterparts to identify biological control agents for such pests.

- *Protecting U.S. investments in migratory species habitats.* The Forest Service works with international counterparts to address habitat issues at both ends of the journey for migratory species.

Ecosystem Services

Ecosystem services are goods and services that we derive from forests and grasslands that are often not valued in the marketplace. Forests and grasslands are valued for basic goods, such as food and wood fiber. But these ecosystems also deliver important services that are often perceived to be free and limitless—air and water purification, flood and climate regulation, biodiversity, and scenic landscapes, for example.

According to one international study, 60 percent of the worldwide ecosystem services evaluated in the study are being degraded or used unsustainably.

The Forest Service is working to advance market-based approaches to conservation and stewardship. Agency research programs provide information on the measurement, monitoring, and valuation of ecosystem services. The National Forest System (NFS) delivers multiple ecosystem services and can serve as a natural laboratory for informing scientific knowledge and policy. State and Private Forestry encourages market-based approaches through public outreach and education, technical assistance to private forest landowners and forestry professionals, and innovative partnerships.

New Perspectives in Urban Forests

More than 80 percent of the Nation's population now lives in cities, suburbs, and towns. This urbanization is part of a global trend that is placing great stress on vital life-sustaining ecological systems. Critical concerns include air quality, water quality and quantity, energy consumption, recreational opportunities, fish and wildlife habitat, and human physical and mental health. The agency has responded with research to evaluate environmental and land use changes in and around urban centers and with collaborative efforts to address these changes. Forest Service activities and initiatives include the following:

- The first-ever national assessment of the Nation's urban forests.

- A science-based urban forest research program conducted in cooperation with the State foresters and other partners.

- An intensive study of the urban ecosystems of several major cities in cooperation with various partners and cosponsors, including the National Science Foundation, U.S. Environmental Protection Agency, and U.S. Department of Energy.

- Urban forest health monitoring demonstrations in selected cities around the country.

- Technical and financial assistance to States and communities to strengthen urban forest and related natural resource management efforts.

- Partnerships with national organizations, such as the Sustainable Urban Forest Coalition, to promote research, tools, model ordinances, and best practices for managing sustainable, healthy urban trees and forests that yield multiple benefits.

Partnerships

The breadth and scope of conservation efforts in the United States exceed the capability of a single organization. The Forest Service recognizes the challenge and actively seeks to engage others in cooperative conservation. By working with partners, the Forest Service expands its capability to participate in conservation through stewardship, research, and intergovernmental coordination.

State foresters are Forest Service partners who work with the agency to provide technical and financial assistance to nonindustrial private forest landowners and to communities. Communities and tribes with treaty-reserved rights and reservation lands within and adjacent to the national forests are also vital partners. They are dependent on the forests and grasslands for special forest products, botanicals, water, livelihoods, recreation, and quality of life, and they bring important knowledge and resources that improve the health of our forests. We work with all of these partners and with local governments and communities to restore and maintain ecosystem health, economic resiliency, and public safety.

An especially important group of partners consists of those who perform essential work for the Forest Service. The Forest Service provides numerous part-time employment, training, education, and volunteer opportunities. Thousands of people work to "make a difference" in sustaining the Nation's forests and to share in the Forest Service's mission. Without them, the agency could not accomplish its work in "caring for the land and serving people."

Management Processes

Planning

Managing the Nation's forests and grasslands requires the complex integration of several levels of planning and cooperation with State and local planning efforts. These levels are defined below.

- *Strategic planning* takes place at the highest level and identifies strategic priorities for the agency that are implemented over a period of time through annual agency budgets. The strategic priorities are based on national assessments of natural resources and are responsive to social and political trends.

- *Business planning* by national programs, regions, research stations, and the Northeastern Area translates the broad strategic direction into the regionally specific work that contributes to the agency's mission.

- *Unit planning* (e.g., land and resource management plans for national forests and grasslands) provides an inventory of resources and their present conditions on a particular management unit. This inventory, coupled with the desired future condition for the resources, is the basis for annual work planning and budgeting.

- *Annual work planning* identifies the projects that all units propose for funding within a fiscal year. This level of planning involves the final application of strategic direction into a unit's annual budget to move its resources toward its desired future condition.

Monitoring

It is essential that the Forest Service track resource conditions and human activities over time to effectively manage the Nation's forests and grasslands. The measures or indicators used for monitoring will vary depending on the level of planning to which they apply.

The Forest Service also conducts financial and performance monitoring to track whether funds are used for their intended purpose and assess results or outcomes of work activity.

Employee Principles

In addition to focusing on the planning and monitoring issues discussed previously, the Forest Service also focuses on core aspects of workforce management. The principles presented below ensure that our employees and the public we serve are treated with full respect and trust.

- **Civil rights.** In valuing the knowledge and skill contributions of a highly diverse workforce, agency managers are committed to preventing discrimination both in program delivery and in workplace practices.

- **Career management and skill development.** The agency recognizes that maintaining and improving the work skills of its diverse workforce improves program efficiency.

- **Safety and occupational health.** Major priorities of the agency are protecting the public and employees from natural dangers and ensuring a safe and healthy place for employees to work.

- **Customer service.** Service is implicit in the agency's name and motto. A major principle of the Forest Service is instilling and maintaining the spirit of customer service in every employee. It is the job of every employee to offer exceptional customer service.

As the agency moves into the next planning cycle, it will continue to focus on its strategic priorities as described in the strategic goals and objectives presented in the next section.

Goal 1. Restore, Sustain, and Enhance the Nation's Forests and Grasslands
(USDA Objectives 6.1, 6.3, 6.4)

Outcome: Forests and grasslands with the capacity to maintain their health, productivity, diversity, and resistance to unnaturally severe disturbance.

The national forests and grasslands were established to protect the land, secure favorable waterflows, and provide a sustainable supply of goods and services. Even before the creation of the Forest Service, the USDA was responsible for providing land management assistance to the States and private forest landowners. Over the past century, the Forest Service has achieved a balance between providing land stewardship services and meeting public demands for various uses of the NFS. Despite past successes, challenges persist. In recent years, people have become more aware of forest disturbance. The increasing extent and frequency of uncharacteristically severe wildland fires and insect and disease outbreaks have been of particular concern to the public, the Administration, Congress, and land management agencies.

To achieve this goal and restore the resiliency of our forest and grassland ecosystems, the Forest Service will focus its efforts on the following objectives.

Objective 1.1
Reduce the risk to communities and natural resources from wildfire.

a. **Performance Measure:** Number and percentage of acres treated to restore fire-adapted ecosystems that are (1) moved toward desired conditions and (2) maintained in desired conditions.
   1. *2006 Baseline:* 991,000 acres (39 percent); *2012 Target:* 1.6 million acres (40 percent).
   2. *2006 Baseline:* 830,000 acres (33 percent); *2012 Target:* 2 million acres (50 percent).

b. **Performance Measure:** Number of acres brought into stewardship contracts. *2006 Baseline:* 57,500 acres; *2012 Target:* 150,000 acres.

Objective 1.2
Suppress wildfires efficiently and effectively.

a. **Performance Measure:** Percentage of fires not contained in initial attack that exceed a stratified cost index.
2006 Baseline: 24 percent; *2012 Target:* 14 percent.

Objective 1.3
Build community capacity to suppress and reduce losses from wildfires.

a. **Performance Measure:** Percentage of acres treated in the wildland-urban interface that have been identified in community wildfire protection plans or equivalent plans.
2006 Baseline: 17 percent; *2012 Target:* 50 percent.

Objective 1.4
Reduce adverse impacts from invasive and native species, pests, and diseases.

a. **Performance Measure:** Percentage of priority acres restored and/or protected from invasive species on Federal and cooperative program lands.
2002 Baseline: 90 percent; *2012 Target*: 90 percent.

Objective 1.5
Restore and maintain healthy watersheds and diverse habitats.

a. **Performance Measure:** Percentage of watershed in class 1 condition.
2005 Baseline: 30 percent; *2012 Target:* 32 percent.

b. **Performance Measure:** Acres and miles of terrestrial and aquatic habitat restored consistent with forest plan direction.
2005 Baseline: 642,000 terrestrial acres; *2012 Target:* Increase by 5 percent annually.
2005 Baseline: 4,600 stream miles; *2012 Target:* Increase by 5 percent annually.
2005 Baseline: 18,000 lake acres; *2012 Target*: Increase by 5 percent annually.

c. **Performance Measure:** Percentage of acres needing reforestation or timber stand improvement that were treated.
2005 Baseline: 13 percent; *2012 Target:* 20 percent.

Means and Strategies for Accomplishing Goal 1

- Develop and apply detection, prediction, prevention, mitigation, treatment, and restoration methods, technologies, and strategies for addressing disturbances (e.g., wildfire, pests, extreme events).

- Provide technical and financial assistance to communities to reduce their risk from wildfire through neighborhood preparation, prevention, education, increased fire suppression self-sufficiency, and community wildfire protection plans.

- Assess the ecological and socioeconomic impacts of global environmental change to the Nation's forests and grasslands.

- Improve firefighting training programs for the safe, efficient, and effective initial attack and suppression of wildfire.

- Use best management practices and scientific results when implementing ground-disturbing or management activities.

- Maintain resilient land and water conditions at the watershed level and restore deteriorated lands and waters (e.g., abandoned mine lands).

- Develop and implement conservation strategies to conserve endangered, threatened, and other at-risk species.

- Monitor the status of congressionally designated areas and manage them to protect and enhance the values for which they were designated.

- Improve the efficiency of land management treatments that provide for the use of woody biomass.

- Establish and implement environmental management systems on national forests, grasslands, and prairies.

Goal 2. Provide and Sustain Benefits to the American People (USDA Objective 6.3)

Outcome: Forests and grasslands with sufficient long-term multiple socioeconomic benefits to meet the needs of society.

This strategic goal and its associated objectives focus on the portion of the agency's mission related to sustaining the productivity of the Nation's forests and grasslands to meet the needs of present and future generations. Our forests and grasslands contain abundant natural resources and opportunities that help meet the demands and needs of the American people. Sustainable management of these resources ensures that the availability of goods and services continues into the future and that land productivity is maintained.

The forest reserves that formed the base of the NFS were created in 1897 for the purposes of improving and protecting land, securing favorable waterflows, and providing a continuous supply of timber. The Multiple-Use Sustained Yield Act of 1960 directed that the national forests be administered for outdoor recreation, rangeland, timber, watershed, and wildlife and fish. National forest management provides a variety of use opportunities while maintaining wildlife diversity, supplies of wood products, energy sources and transmission infrastructure, wildlife and domestic livestock forage, water supplies, and other goods and services.

Primarily through State and Private Forestry programs, the Forest Service provides technical and financial assistance for natural resource management and the sustainable use of resources on non-Federal lands in the United States. International technical assistance is also provided. Our research provides a solid scientific foundation for the sustainable management of forests and grasslands and improvements in the use and marketing of forest products and services.

During this strategic planning period, the following objectives will be our major focus for accomplishing this goal.

Objective 2.1
Provide a reliable supply of forest products over time that (1) is consistent with achieving desired conditions on NFS lands and (2) helps maintain or create processing capacity and infrastructure in local communities.

a. **Performance Measure:** Amount of wood fiber provided each year to help meet the Nation's demand for forest products in an environmentally sustainable manner.
2006 Baseline: 5.4 million CCF[1]; *2012 Target:* 8.0 million CCF.

b. **Performance Measure:** Number of green tons and/or volume of woody biomass from hazardous fuel reduction and restoration treatments on Federal land that are made available through permits, contracts, grants, agreements, or the equivalent. *2006 Baseline:* N/A[2]; *2012 Target:* 2.7 million green tons.

Objective 2.2
Provide a reliable supply of rangeland products over time that (1) is consistent with achieving desired conditions on NFS lands and (2) helps support ranching in local communities.

a. **Performance Measure:** Acres of national forests and grasslands under grazing permit that are sustainably managed for all rangeland products. *2006 Baseline:* 81.56 million acres; *2012 Target:* 81.56 million acres.

Objective 2.3
Help meet energy resource needs.

a. **Performance Measure:** Percentage of land Special Use Permit applications for energy-related facilities that are completed within prescribed timeframes. *2005 Baseline:* 50 percent; *2012 Target:* 50 percent.

b. **Performance Measure:** Percentage of energy-mineral applications that are processed within prescribed timeframes. *2006 Baseline:* 45 percent; *2012 Target:* 55 percent.

Objective 2.4
Promote market-based conservation and stewardship of ecosystem services.

a. **Performance Measure:** Number of States that have agreements with the Forest Service to help private forest landowners market ecosystem services. *2006 Baseline:* 1 State; *2012 Target:* 14 States.

---

[1] One "CCF" is 100 cubic feet.
[2] The initial collection of data for this performance measure commenced at the beginning of fiscal year 2007.

Means and Strategies for Accomplishing Goal 2

- Provide access to natural resources to meet the Nation's economic, social, and environmental needs.

- Develop and disseminate technologies and market strategies to produce energy and products from renewable forest and rangeland resources.

- Monitor changes in U.S. natural resource-based markets in response to globalization and provide information to decisionmakers and the public.

- Inventory, model, and monitor potential and actual levels of sustainable forest products from forest land to strengthen forest product markets and improve the use of wood products.

- Develop tools and provide technical and financial assistance to increase the production of energy from woody biomass.

- Effectively manage and maintain the infrastructure to support the products, services, and uses of NFS lands.

- Increase the efficiency of decisions about Special Use Permits for NFS lands.

- Target landowner planning, technical, and financial assistance programs to priority forest areas.

- Help State forestry agencies and other partners monitor, evaluate, and advance market-based approaches to enhance and protect ecosystem services on private and community lands.

Goal 3. Conserve Open Space
(USDA Objective 6.3)

Outcome: Maintain the environmental, social, and economic benefits of forests and grasslands by reducing and mitigating their conversion to other uses.

Open space provides many environmental, social, and economic benefits to rural and urban communities. Undeveloped forests and grasslands, including working farms, ranches, and timber lands, help protect water quality, conserve native wildlife, and provide renewable timber and nontimber products, places to recreate, and scenic beauty. These "green spaces" elevate home values and generate jobs and economic vitality. Current population growth trends show a steady loss of these vital open spaces to developed uses.

The Forest Service, in partnership with State forestry agencies, annually helps communities develop sustainable urban and community forestry programs. Communities use urban forest management plans to help mitigate the impacts of existing and new developments on open space. Urban forest management plans, derived from urban tree and forest resource inventories, include protection and management recommendations that become key components of community development and open-space planning.

During this strategic planning period, the following objectives will be our major focus for accomplishing this goal.

Objective 3.1
Protect forests and grasslands from conversion to other uses.

a. **Performance Measure:** Acres of environmentally important forests and grasslands protected from conversion.
    2006 Baseline: 1.36 million acres; *2012 Target:* 2 million acres.

Objective 3.2
Help private landowners and communities maintain and manage their land as sustainable forests and grasslands.

a. **Performance Measure:** Acres of nonindustrial private forest land that are being managed sustainably under forest stewardship management plans.
    2007 Baseline: 1.76 million acres; *2012 Target:* 2 million acres.

Means and Strategies for Accomplishing Goal 3

- Monitor land use change and develop tools to predict and evaluate the interaction between public lands and other ownerships across the rural-urban continuum.

- Develop and disseminate management strategies to mitigate habitat loss and fragmentation impacts on plant and animal communities at the landscape level.

- Promote strategic conservation and environmentally sensitive development planning in and adjacent to communities to preserve and restore forested landscapes and urban tree cover.

- Identify those lands that are most at risk for conversion and those that are most important for providing public benefits and take the following actions:

  - Acquire land adjacent to or near NFS lands through purchase, conveyance, boundary adjustments, and donations to protect priority forest areas.

  - Protect private forests in partnership with States through permanent conservation easements and land acquisition (e.g., the Forest Legacy Program).

- Continue NFS grazing permits to maintain associated base properties as sustainable working ranches.

- Provide technical assistance to landowners to accomplish the following goals:

  - Increase the economic viability of private forest lands with income derived from the marketing of forest products, woody biomass, ecosystem services, and recreation.

  - Develop forest stewardship plans to identify sustainable management goals and practices for landowners' land.

  - Increase landowners' understanding of forest taxation and estate-planning strategies.

- Promote community planning for sustainable tourism and recreation that provide economic incentives to maintain open space lands.

- Provide educational, technical, and financial assistance to urban communities and urban/suburban landowners to restore environmental services through urban forestry, agroforestry, and "green infrastructure" approaches.

- Coordinate national forest plan revisions with local land-use plans to minimize the impacts of new and existing developments on NFS resources and management activities.

Goal 4. Sustain and Enhance Outdoor Recreation Opportunities (USDA Objective 6.3)

Outcome: A variety of high-quality outdoor recreational opportunities on the Nation's forests and grasslands are available to the public.

The Forest Service is challenged with sustaining adequate high-quality outdoor recreational experiences to meet the Nation's needs while maintaining the ecological integrity of national forests and grasslands. The Nation's population is projected to increase by nearly 50 percent by the middle of this century. The combination of increasing populations and the continued decline of public access to privately owned forest land creates extensive pressure on public lands to provide more recreational opportunities.

If public lands are to provide additional recreational benefits without unacceptable resource impacts, we must emphasize effective management solutions that have a solid scientific foundation. The condition of the land, recreation facilities, and transportation infrastructure, including off-highway-vehicle access, must be considered if we expect to preserve high-quality recreation experiences. We must maintain specially designated protected areas. We must continue to work with our partner volunteers, nongovernmental organizations, other agencies, and the private sector if we are to achieve acceptable results.

During this strategic planning period, the following objectives will be our major focus for accomplishing this goal.

Objective 4.1
Improve the quality and availability of outdoor recreation experiences.

a. **Performance Measure:** Percentage of recreation sites maintained to standard.
    2005 Baseline: 65 percent; *2012 Target:* 81 percent.

b. **Performance Measure:** Percentage of total recreation capacity at developed recreation sites that meets accessibility standards.
    2006 Baseline: 10 percent; *2012 Target:* 30 percent.

c. **Performance Measure:** Percentage of trails that meet national quality standards.
    2006 Baseline: 60 percent; *2012 Target:* 60 percent.

d. **Performance Measure:** Percentage of customers who are satisfied with recreational facilities, services, and settings.
    2004 Baseline: 80 percent; *2012 Target:* 85 percent.

e. **Performance Measure:** Percentage of road system intended for passenger-car use that is suitable for passenger-car use.[3]
   2006 Baseline: 29 percent; *2012 Target:* 75 percent.

Objective 4.2
Secure legal entry to national forest lands and waters.

a. **Performance Measure:** Percentage of high-priority access rights-of-way acquired.
   2007 Baseline: 90 percent; *2012 Target:* 95 percent.

Objective 4.3
Improve the management of off-highway vehicle use.

a. **Performance Measure:** Percentage of NFS lands covered by new motor vehicle use maps reflecting a designated-use system of roads, trails, and areas.
   2002 Baseline: 0 percent; *2012 Target:* 100 percent.

[3] The road miles intended for passenger car use will be redefined in new unit-based travel management plans (also referenced in Objective 4.3) (ref: 36 CFR 12.55).

Means and Strategies for Accomplishing Goal 4

- Provide tools, guidance, and resource management to provide safe recreation use and to prevent or mitigate the ecological impacts of recreation activities (including off-highway vehicle impacts).

- Improve our understanding of the relationship between the quality of the recreation experience and the quality of the environment to help managers optimize recreational opportunities and investments.

- Develop the tools necessary to protect and sustain designated wilderness areas and the ecological and social values derived from designated wilderness areas.

- Develop information about visitor trends, behavior, and experiences to help managers and communities provide the recreation services and benefits that visitors seek.

- Provide recreational opportunities consistent with an area's physical, biological, and social characteristics and capabilities.

- Acquire and provide appropriate access to recreational opportunities.

- Efficiently and effectively manage and maintain recreational opportunity infrastructure while protecting public health and safety (including facility reconstruction and decommissioning, where appropriate).

- Maintain and improve a user-fee program.

- Use private, nongovernmental, and interagency partnerships to accomplish collaborative community recreation/tourism plans.

Goal 5. Maintain Basic Management Capabilities of the Forest Service
(USDA Objectives 6.1, 6.3, 6.4)

Outcome: Administrative facilities, information systems, and landownership management with the capacity to support a wide range of natural resource challenges.

Natural resources are affected by a wide range of forces, including natural events, overuse, and various management activities. The Forest Service maintains a workforce with the skills and capabilities to deal with the impacts of these events. Reliable information, quality facilities, and land protection are necessary to effectively manage natural resources in a perpetual state of change.

During this strategic planning period, the following objectives will be our major focus for accomplishing this goal.

Objective 5.1
Improve accountability through effective strategic and land-management planning and efficient use of data and technology in resource management.

a. **Performance Measure:** Percentage of selected data in information systems that is current to standard.
   2006 Baseline: 44 percent; *2012 Target:* 100 percent.

Objective 5.2
Improve the administration of national forest lands and facilities in support of the agency's mission.

a. **Performance Measure:** Percentage of administrative facilities that are being maintained to standard.
   2006 Baseline: 64 percent; *2012 Target:* 75 percent.

b. **Performance Measure:** Percentage of newly reported encroachments and title claims administered to standard.
   2006 Baseline: 60 percent; *2012 Target:* 90 percent.

Means and Strategies for Accomplishing Goal 5

- Recruit and train personnel to develop and maintain strong technical and leadership skills in Forest Service program areas to meet current and future challenges.

- Increase interagency efforts such as "Service First" to jointly develop and share employee skills across agency lines.

- Retrain existing employees or recruit new personnel to meet new workforce needs when the current workforce does not possess necessary skills.

- Refine career development guidance and training programs for entry-level professionals.

- Develop tools and provide knowledge management training to Forest Service employees to improve their capacity to develop and sustain partnerships.

- Continue to cooperate with other Federal, State, and local government units, tribes, and private-sector partners.

- Manage and protect the public's ownership rights and the interests of the NFS.

Goal 6. Engage Urban America With Forest Service Programs (USDA Objective 6.3)

Outcome: Broader access by Americans to the long-term environmental, social, economic, and other types of benefits provided by the Forest Service.

The three branches of the Forest Service collectively contribute to an integrated program of natural resources stewardship to better connect urban residents to the value of well-managed public and private forested lands and improve their quality of life. The Forest Service works to promote understanding and beneficial management of the urban forest. We support conservation education, community "greening" efforts, and programs that provide youth with opportunities to volunteer in tree planting and urban forest inventory activities in their neighborhoods and visit national forests and grasslands. We work closely with a variety of partners at the Federal, State, and local levels to improve our understanding of what urban residents think of and want from their local parks, nearby woodlands, and national forests to build productive relationships with urban neighbors. Through partnerships among the Forest Service, other Federal agencies, and State and local organizations, we build connections between rural and urban communities.

During this strategic planning period, the following objectives will be our major focus for accomplishing this goal.

Objective 6.1
Promote conservation education to increase environmental literacy through partnerships with groups that benefit and educate urban populations.

a. **Performance Measure:** Number of people who annually participate in Forest Service environmental literacy programs and activities.
2005 Baseline: 2.5 million people; *2012 Target:* 3.2 million people.

Objective 6.2
Improve the management of urban and community forests to provide a wide range of public benefits.

a. **Performance Measure:** Number of communities with developing or established urban and community forestry programs resulting from Forest Service assistance.
2006 Baseline: 6,564 communities; *2012 Target:* 10,000 communities.

Means and Strategies for Accomplishing Goal 6

- Continue urban forest inventory and analysis to monitor the health and benefits of ecological and social services of urban forests and more effectively manage these complex landscapes.

- Develop and disseminate strategies and options such as "green infrastructure" to effectively manage resources to maintain environmental quality and services in urban and urbanizing landscapes.

- Help communities increase professional urban forestry staffing, ordinances, management plans, and local advisory and advocacy groups for managing forest resources in cities, suburbs, and towns.

- Develop and disseminate tools to ensure that urban trees and forests are strategically planned and managed to maximize ecosystem services and benefits.

- Engage partners and educators in the development, distribution, and use of high-quality conservation education materials and interpretive programs.

- Develop methods to measure environmental literacy and techniques to engage urban residents in the management of urban forests.

- Improve access by urban Americans to Forest Service resources and information.

- Develop partnerships with nontraditional partners to engage urban and underserved audiences.

Goal 7. Provide Science-Based Applications and Tools for Sustainable Natural Resources Management
(USDA Objective 6.3)

Outcome: Management decisions are informed by the best available science-based knowledge and tools.

The Forest Service provides science and technology solutions for clients' and partners' priority issues in ways they find effective and useful for sustainably managing forests and grasslands.

To accomplish this goal, Research and Development (R&D) and Technology and Development (T&D) Centers will focus on the following objectives in this strategic planning period.

Objective 7.1
Increase the use of applications and tools developed by Forest Service R&D stations and T&D centers.

a. **Performance Measure:** Customer satisfaction with R&D products and services.
2005 Baseline: American Customer Satisfaction Index (ACSI)[4] score of 72; *2012 Target:* ACSI score of 75.

b. **Performance Measure:** Number of patent applications filed, based on station and center discoveries, developments, and applications.
2005 Baseline: 10 applications; *2012 Target:* 13 applications.

---

[4] The American Customer Satisfaction Index assesses the satisfaction of private and other external customers with the relevance, usefulness, and accessibility of Research and Development products and services.

Means and Strategies for Accomplishing Goal 7

- Develop and make available cost-effective methods for transferring scientific information, technologies, methods, and applications.

- Provide information and science-based tools that are used by managers and policymakers.

- Develop and implement effective processes for engaging users in all phases of R&D study development.

- Develop and deploy analysis and decision-support systems.

- Develop tools for evaluating the efficiency and effectiveness of alternative management practices.

- Ensure that current resource information is available to address the strategic, tactical, and operational business requirements of the agency.

External Factors That Impact the Accomplishment of the Goals and Objectives

Factors beyond the control of the Forest Service that could affect progress towards accomplishing these long-term goals and objectives include the following:

- Extreme weather, climate fluctuations, and environmental change beyond the natural range of forest and grassland variability that affect ecological productivity and resilience.

- Legal or regulatory constraints or changes that affect management activities, available options, or program resources.

- Incomplete, untimely, or conflicting information that reduces managerial efficiency and effectiveness.

- Independent actions by external groups or individuals, including landowners, that affect forest and grassland management or Forest Service objectives.

- Demographic shifts or changes in stakeholder perceptions that result in unanticipated shifts in expectations.

- Unpredictable economic fluctuations that change market conditions and human behaviors.

- International crises or homeland security issues that alter domestic program accomplishments or public needs.

Business Foundation

The Forest Service is committed to providing efficient, effective administrative support to its programs, enabling its employees to deliver on their core mission of sustainable resource management. We continue to improve our financial accountability, provide efficient management of program resources, promote a safe and healthy work environment, develop a diverse workforce, and further implement sound business practices.

Administrative management of the Forest Service is complex and ever changing. The Business Operations staffs must continuously improve their partnership with field managers and employees in an interactive, virtual environment. We accomplish this goal by delivering services in a professional, knowledgeable, friendly, and cost-effective manner. We are committed to serving the ever-changing needs of our many partners, customers, and the public.

Human Resources

The Forest Service continues to enhance its most valuable asset—its employees—to ensure that we bring a diversity of ideas and skills to the increasingly diverse customer base. Ours is a workplace that respects, appreciates, and values individual differences and uses those differences to improve organizational performance, customer service, and workplace relations. We are committed to developing our employees to their fullest potential to ensure a workforce that is successful in today's competitive environment.

To ensure that the Forest Service has the best skills, we continue to do the following:

- Refine and implement a strategic workforce plan.
- Provide state-of the-art training at all career levels.
- Require new employees to attend a comprehensive orientation program.

We are dedicated to reducing our employees' and the public's exposure to hazards that threaten their safety and health, recognizing that our business has the potential to expose people to hazardous situations every day.

Human Capital Management processes are being reengineered and centralized to provide more efficient service to all employees in the agency from one location. This effort ensures that business policies, processes, and organizations enhance performance and service delivery of human resource functions. Efficiencies reduce costs and redundancies, and they increase consistency of functions across the agency.

Financial Performance

The Forest Service continues agencywide efforts to improve financial management, demonstrating our ability to effectively and efficiently safeguard and manage public funds and property. The agency is focused on redesigning and streamlining many financial management policies, processes, and procedures. We are gaining further efficiencies by locating financial support services in a single service center. Centralizing these processes helps the Forest Service standardize transaction processes and required reports. This effort enables regions, research stations, and field offices to focus less on time-consuming administrative tasks and more on core business activities.

To demonstrate our performance in improving financial management, we will do the following:

- Maintain an "unqualified" audit opinion from the Office of the Inspector General through FY 2012 and beyond.

- Comply with Office of Management and Budget (OMB) Circular A-123 to eliminate all material weaknesses in financial processes.

- Consolidate our financial and performance monitoring systems into a single Performance Accountability System (PAS).

- Improve financial reporting processes and provide transparency and accountability for administrative costs.

Electronic Government

We continue to improve our service to the public through the application of newly available information technology infrastructures and skills. Information required for agency accountability and for more effective employees is now available electronically through the Information Services Organization (ISO). Our electronic government goal is to provide more efficient service to meet Forest Service computing needs.

By improving our electronic delivery system we are able to do the following:

- Give our employees access to more self-service options.

- Share data with our customers and the public in a more effective and timely manner.

- Consolidate internal planning, budget, and performance information in our "Managing for Results" Web site.

Competitive Sourcing

The Forest Service will aim to improve its performance through efficient competition between public and private sources. We will implement the competitive sourcing initiative in a reasonable and rational manner to realize significant cost savings and better align our workforce with the agency mission. We will make every effort to reach and evaluate a full spectrum of sources to achieve these efficiencies.

Budget and Performance Integration

The Forest Service integrates planning and budgeting with performance monitoring throughout the budget formulation and execution process. Planning and budget staffs work with executives and program staffs to identify funding priorities within the agency's strategic goals. Through the PAS we track our progress in achieving desired outcomes at all stages, from project planning to final reporting.

We evaluate our programs regularly and incorporate the results of those evaluations into management and funding decisions. We rely heavily on the results of Program Assessment Rating Tool (PART) reviews and Research and Development Investment Criteria (see the section with this title) reviews to modify and direct future budget decisions.

Civil Rights

The Forest Service delivers progressive Equal Employment Opportunity and Equal Opportunity programs. Our three Civil Rights strategic objectives target regulatory compliance, prevention of discrimination, and education about discriminatory practices. The objectives of prevention and education focus on the spirit as well as the intent of the law, and they move the agency beyond a focus on compliance. We have a revitalized program of outreach, recruitment, and retention of people in key groups following results of a survey on diversity. We provide a series of tools to help employees better understand diversity and civil rights issues in an effort to prevent discrimination.

We are committed to complying with all Equal Employment Opportunity Commission regulations and directives, as well as USDA directives and strategic plans. The new Civil Rights Accountability Policy and Procedures (USDA regulation DR4300-010) direction strengthens existing civil rights policies and encourages us to work to resolve complaints at the earliest possible opportunity.

Under this regulation, managers and supervisors are directly accountable for maintaining a civil rights program that accomplishes strategic civil rights goals. Annual performance appraisals for managers and supervisors must now include an evaluation of their contributions to civil rights and equal opportunity. When discrimination, retaliation, civil rights violations, or related misconduct occurs, managers and supervisors are held accountable for taking appropriate disciplinary or corrective action.

Research and Development Investment Criteria

Forest Service R&D provides a strong scientific foundation for resource management decisions by drawing from natural resource and adaptive management expertise, decades of data obtained from its experimental forests and grasslands, a network of strong and productive partnerships, and a national system of inventory and monitoring plots. We evaluate our programs using Investment Criteria developed by the OMB and Office of Science and Technology Policy. These criteria help ensure delivery of the best available science to resource managers.

All R&D programs will be reviewed on a 5-year cycle by teams of external experts to quantitatively assess the relevance, quality, and performance of each program reviewed, with a target rating of satisfactory or excellent on 100 percent of its programs.

Customer satisfaction with the relevance, usefulness, and accessibility of R&D products and services will be monitored using the nationally recognized American Customer Satisfaction Index (ACSI). It is an objective, independently administered survey, and R&D will contract for this survey every 3 years. Targets are ACSI scores of 73 for 2009 and 75 by 2012.

Information derived from the reviews and surveys will enable R&D managers to identify ways to improve customer service and to make better informed budget and program management decisions.

Program Evaluations

The Government Performance and Results Act of 1993 requires agencies to develop strategic plans containing a description of the program evaluations used in establishing or revising general goals and objectives, with a schedule for future program evaluations. The Forest Service engages in the program evaluations described below. Most of the evaluations are applied to all aspects of agency programs, but not necessarily within the same year. Schedules are established each year so that, in a 3-to-5-year span, all programs are reviewed. The review schedule for any given year is shared agencywide in the budget program direction issued at the beginning of the fiscal year.

Evaluations Used To Revise Goals and Objectives

In 2005, the Forest Service chartered interdisciplinary teams to complete integrated goal strategies associated with the *USDA Forest Service Strategic Plan for Fiscal Years 2004–2008*. Using a standardized methodology, integrated strategies were developed to facilitate implementation of the goals. In addition, the strategies included an evaluation of the goals, objectives, and performance measures to be considered during revision of the strategic plan.

The evaluations required recommendations for future goals and objectives with identification of associated outcome statements, outcome measures, efficiency measures, output measures, measure baselines, and projected targets related to the potentially revised goals, objectives, and performance measures. When determining the suitability of proposed goals, objectives, and performance measures for the FY 2007–12 strategic plan update, we considered the developed information and recommendations.

The USDA Office of Inspector General completed an external review of Forest Service implementation of the Government Performance and Results Act in 2005. We also considered the useful findings on performance measures, internal controls, and program evaluations that were provided in the report when updating the strategic plan.

The process to revise and update strategic direction for the Forest Service includes scanning natural resource and public trends.

Schedule of Future Program Evaluations

The Forest Service regularly conducts program evaluations at various levels of the organization from the executive level to individual project or site reviews. The following schedule identifies significant evaluations projected over the next 5 years.

As necessary, the agency will conduct additional studies and evaluations as directed by agency leadership, the Administration, or Congress.

Future Program Evaluation Schedule

Evaluations/Analyses	General Scope	Methodology	Timetable
Environmental Management System	National forest unit level evaluation	External review	
R&D Program Peer Review	National level	Comprehensive external subject-matter specialist review of strategic program area	Every 5 years or 20% each year (100% of R&D Program)
R&D Administrative Review	Washington Office and research station level	Review of administrative functions by panel of Forest Service personnel and external partners and collaborators	Periodically
R&D Project Review	Research work unit level	Internal review of work units and charters	Every 5 years
Regional Activity reviews	Chief's review	Integrated review of joint region and R&D programs to evaluate mission delivery	Periodically
Civil Rights Title VI and VII reviews	Program reviews	Regions, stations, and area reviews	Periodically
Maintenance reviews (fleet, roads, structures)	Program reviews	Regions, stations, and area reviews	Periodically
Integrated reviews of programs with partners	Review of programs under agreements or memoranda	Program and partner field reviews	Periodically
Business Management Audits (budgeting, accounting, fund management)	Program reviews of the business functions and service centers	Regions, stations, and area reviews	Periodically
OMB PART	Use PART to assess the management and results of selected goals and programs	Develop responses to a series of questions assessing program management and performance	Annually with all strategic goals reviewed every 5 years
Forest and Rangeland Renewable Resources Planning Act assessments of U.S. natural resources	Evaluate status of America's natural resources and identify trends in condition and uses of those resources	Independent technical documents of emerging issues and analyses of natural resource conditions, present and future, by Nation's scientists	Every 10 years with interim 5-year updates (complete assessment)

www.ingramcontent.com/pod-product-compliance
Lightning Source LLC
Chambersburg PA
CBHW082202290526
45794CB00008B/3389